EDIBLE
numbers

Jennifer Vogel Bass

Roaring Brook Press
New York

1 pea pod

Sugar Daddy

2 pea pods

Blue Podded

Golden Sweet Snow

1 apple

Cortland

3 apples

Golden Delicious

Granny Smith

Golden Russett

1 cucumber

Kirby

4 cucumbers

Dragon's Egg

Asian Burpless

Sikkim

Lemon

1 potato

Idaho

5 potatoes

Yukon Gold

Blossom

Russian Blue

Adirondack Blue

Adirondack Red

1 pear

Bartlett

6 pears

Red Bartlett

Olympic Giant Asian

Bosc

Shinko Asian

Red Anjou

Seckel

1 pepper

Ace

7 peppers

King Arthur

Gourmet

Islander

Cubanelle

Flavorburst

Bianca

Sweet Chocolate

1 mushroom

Button

8 mushrooms

Wood Ear

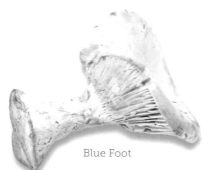

Blue Foot

Nameko

Pom Pom Blanc

Morel

Chanterelle

Trumpet

Hen of the Woods

1 squash

Partenon zucchini

9 squashes

Geode

One-Ball zucchini

Flying Saucer Pattypan

Early Golden Crookneck

Patisson Blanc

Zephyr

Eight-Ball zucchini

Avocado

Yellow Pattypan

1 tomato

Beefsteak

10 tomatoes

Kumato

Berkeley Tie-Dye

Striped Roman

Yellow
Mortgage
Lifter

Pink
German

Green
Sausage

White Queen

Green Zebra

Striped Cavern

Cherokee Purple

1 eggplant

Black Beauty

11 eggplants

Machiaw

Gretel

Louisiana Long Green

Turkish Orange

Thai Yellow Egg

Barbarella

Aubergine du Burkina Faso

Nipple Fruit

Kermit

Orient Express

Nubia

1 citrus fruit

Navel orange

12 citrus fruits

Meyer lemon

Sumo

Variegated
Pink lemon

Kaffir
lime

Mexican
lime

Yuzu

Ruby Red
grapefruit

Blood orange

Australian Finger lime

Mandarin

Pomelo

Buddha's Hand citron

How many **plums** can you count?
How many **ears of corn** do you see?
How many **watermelons** can you find?
How many **carrots** can you spot?

Snow White carrot

Amarillo watermelon

Green Gage plum

Bicolor corn

Blue Damson plum

Friar plum

Sugarsnax carrot

Blue Jade corn

Santa Rosa plum

Cosmic Purple carrot

Shiro plum

Moon and Stars watermelon

Deep Purple carrot

Ruby Queen corn

French Market carrot

Black Mountain watermelon

Atomic Red carrot

Purple corn

Oaxacan Green Dent corn

Italian Prune plum

Yellowstone carrot

We're counting with
EDIBLE
NUMBERS!

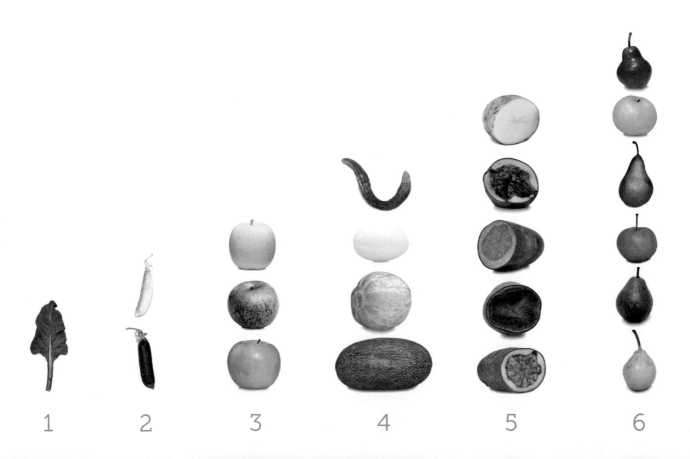

1 2 3 4 5 6

7 8 9 10 11 12

Text and photographs copyright © 2015 by Jennifer Vogel Bass
Published by Roaring Brook Press
Roaring Brook Press is a division of Holtzbrinck Publishing Holdings Limited Partnership
175 Fifth Avenue, New York, New York 10010
mackids.com

Library of Congress Cataloging-in-Publication Data

Bass, Jennifer Vogel, author.
  Edible numbers / Jennifer Vogel Bass. — First edition.
    pages cm
  Summary: "A colorful and delicious counting book featuring an array of
familiar and unfamiliar fruits and vegetables."— Provided by publisher.
  Audience. Ages 2–5.
  ISBN 978-1-62672-003-9 (hardcover)
1. Counting—Juvenile literature. 2. Vegetables—Juvenile literature. 3. Fruit—Juvenile literature. I. Title.
  QA113.B3788 2014
  513.2—dc23
                                                                    2014030955

Roaring Brook Press books may be purchased for business or promotional use. For information on bulk
purchases please contact Macmillan Corporate and Premium Sales Department at (800) 221-7945 x5442
or by email at specialmarkets@macmillan.com.

First edition 2015
Book design by Elizabeth Holden Clark
Printed in China by Macmillan Production (Asia) Ltd., Kowloon Bay, Hong Kong (supplier code 10)

10 9 8 7 6 5 4 3 2 1